Track & Field

track&FIELD

GETTING THE EDGE: CONDITIONING, INJURIES, AND LEGAL & ILLICIT DRUGS

Baseball and Softball

Basketball

Cheerleading

Extreme Sports

Football

Gymnastics

Hockey

Lacrosse

Martial Arts

Soccer

Track & Field

Volleyball

Weightlifting

Wrestling

track
&FIELD

Track & Field

by Gabrielle Vanderhoof

Mason Crest Publishers

MASON CREST PUBLISHERS INC.
370 Reed Road
Broomall, Pennsylvania 19008
(866)MCP-BOOK (toll free)
www.masoncrest.com

First Printing
9 8 7 6 5 4 3 2 1

Library of Congress Cataloging-in-Publication Data

Vanderhoof, Gabrielle.
  Track & field / by Gabrielle Vanderhoof.
     p. cm. — (Getting the edge)
  Includes bibliographical references and index.
  ISBN 978-1-4222-1740-5   ISBN (series) 978-1-4222-1728-3

  1. Track and field—Juvenile literature. 2. Track and field. I. Title. II. Title:
Track and field.
  GV1060.55.V36 2011
  796.42—dc22
                                    2010015261

Produced by Harding House Publishing Service, Inc.
www.hardinghousepages.com
Interior Design by MK Bassett-Harvey.
Cover Design by Torque Advertising + Design.
Printed in the USA by Bang Printing.

The creators of this book have made every effort to provide accurate information, but it should not be used as a substitute for the help and services of trained professionals.

Contents

Introduction

GETTING THE EDGE: CONDITIONING, INJURIES, AND LEGAL & ILLICIT DRUGS is a fourteen-volume series written for young people who are interested in learning about various sports and how to participate in them safely. Each volume examines the history of the sport and the rules of play; it also acts as a guide for prevention and treatment of injuries, and includes instruction on stretching, warming up, and strength training, all of which can help players avoid the most common musculoskeletal injuries. Each volume also includes tips on healthy nutrition for athletes, as well as information on the risks of using performance-enhancing drugs or other illegal substances. GETTING THE EDGE offers ways for readers to healthily and legally improve their performance and gain more enjoyment from playing sports. Young athletes will find these volumes informative and helpful in their pursuit of excellence.

Sports medicine professionals assigned to a sport with which they are not familiar can also benefit from this series. For example, a football athletic trainer may need to provide medical care for a local gymnastics meet. Although the emergency medical principles and action plan would remain the same, the athletic trainer could provide better care for the gymnasts after reading a simple overview of the principles of gymnastics in GETTING THE EDGE.

Although these books offer an overview, they are not intended to be comprehensive in the recognition and management of sports injuries. They should not replace the professional advice of a trainer, doctor, or nutritionist. The text helps the reader appreciate and gain awareness of the sport's history, standard training techniques, common injuries, dietary guidelines,

and the dangers of using drugs to gain an advantage. Reference material and directed readings are provided for those who want to delve further into these subjects.

Written in a direct and easily accessible style, GETTING THE EDGE is an enjoyable series that will help young people learn about sports and sports medicine.

—*Susan Saliba, Ph.D., National Athletic Trainers' Association Education Council*

1
Overview of Track-and-Field

Understanding the Words

The **Celts** were a group of people that occupied lands stretching from the British Isles to Gallatia.

A **stopboard,** used in shot put, is a raised arc placed at the front of the circle, which the competitor is not allowed to touch. It is 4 inches high and 4.3 inches wide.

A **take-off box** is placed at the end of a pole vault runway for athletes to plant their pole into and launch themselves into the air.

Physiology is the study of how the body functions.

The collective sport of track-and-field, as we know it today, began as two separate sports over thousands of years. The ancient Greeks and **Celts** were the first civilizations to turn both track and field, respectively, into competitive activities. Now, centuries later, people are still practicing and competing in these events at many levels all over the globe.

History of Track

The first culture to embrace competitive running was Greece. In 776 B.C.E., at the first Olympic Games, running was the only sport. The runners competed in a variety of sprint and distance events, racing around arenas that were tiny in comparison to modern stadiums.

The Greek Olympics were discontinued in the fourth century C.E., but sprang to life again more than 1,500 years later. Many of the running events we are familiar with today were developed or refined in the nineteenth century, specifically in England. In 1837, many colleges in the country began holding hurdling competitions, and in 1876, the first international cross-country championship was held in England.

As the century progressed, more and more running events were added to the British sporting calendar. The world's first track-and-field competition was held in 1850 at Exeter College, which included many events we still use today, such as distance sprints. In the same year, Oxford University introduced the steeplechase event, and in 1854, new distances were added to already-established sports, such as the 110-meter and 400 meters for the hurdles in 1864.

By the second half of the nineteenth century, competitive running had spread across Europe and into the United States. In 1896, the Olympic Games were reborn, and Athens, the capital city of Greece, was chosen to host the games. Running events were held both inside and outside the stadium. Track events, such as the 100-meter sprint and the 1,500-meter distance run, were

performed on the circular Olympic track, while the marathon event took the runners 25 miles (40 km) around the Greek capital.

History of Field Events

While competitive running originated with the ancient Greeks, field events, such as the javelin and shot put, began with the Celtic people. These activities actually began as survival and warfare skills; javelins were used in combat by around the third millennium B.C.E., and the origins of the shot

The importance that competitive running had in Greek culture is revealed in the artwork found on ancient pottery.

TRACK & FIELD

put date back to prehistory, when heavy rocks were hurled in aggression against animals or other humans. Slowly, these instruments of war became instruments of sport.

Some field events, however, were created as sports. The Celts—a people who spread throughout Europe in the first and second millen-

The ancient Olympics were held here, a location that must have rivaled today's elaborate Olympic events.

nia B.C.E.—were great sporting innovators. The long jump was a part of the Celtic games as far back as 2000 B.C.E. and was also included in the ancient Olympics. Celtic people also introduced a version of the high jump as a competition.

As time progressed, existing field events were refined and new ones created. In the fourteenth century C.E., shot putters developed a new object to throw—iron cannon balls, which are very much like the modern shot put. From the same century, hammer throwing emerged; at the time, the hammer was exactly that—a blacksmith's iron hammer. As for the pole vault, it emerged from a medieval method of crossing ditches and rivers.

Putting It All Together

Until the nineteenth century, track-and-field events were a scattered group of sports, with varying rules and equipment. Field events were standardized in nineteenth-century England in public schools and colleges, with their emphasis on sporting achievement and experimentation. With the revival of the Olympics in 1896, field events took their place alongside running events, and together they became the sport we know today: track-and-field.

By the end of the 1800s, almost all the events we are familiar with today had been established, but they were dominated by men. It would be well into the twentieth century before women were able to compete in these events. The full range of men's running events had entered the Olympics by 1920; men ran the 10,000-meter race in 1912, but it was not until more than 75 years later in 1988, that the same event was run by women. This double standard also existed in field events until recently. The first hammer throw competition for men was held in Paris in 1900, and the first for women in Sydney in 2000.

Modern Track-and-Field Events

FIELD

There are currently eight basic field events: javelin, hammer throw, discus, shot put, pole vault, long jump, triple jump, and high jump. The following descriptions are as they appear in Olympic competition.

Javelin

The javelin event is a simple test of who can throw the farthest, although the javelin must touch the floor point-first to qualify as a legal throw. For men, the javelin is 8 feet 6 inches to 8 feet 10 inches (2.6–2.7 m) long and weighs at

Like many of the track-and-field events, the modern javelin throw shown here has roots in ancient history, where throwing a javelin had practical use in both warfare and hunting.

The modern discus-throwing event also began in ancient Greece.

least 1 pound and 12 ounces (800 g). In the women's event, the javelin is 7 feet 2 inches to 7 feet 6 inches (2.2–2.3 m) long and weighs at least 1 pound 5 ounces (600 g). It is thrown over a course about 330 feet (100 m) long. Judges use long tapes to measure the throw distance from the edge of the stopboard to the landing point. Depending on the number of competitors in the event, the athlete will throw either three or six times.

Discus

The discus is a challenging, technical event, requiring timing, balance, and accuracy. Two sizes and weights of discus are used: the men's weighs 4 pounds 6 ounces (2 kg), measures about 8 3/4 inches (219–221 mm) in diameter and is 2 inches (44 mm) thick. The women's equivalent is half the weight, about 7 inches (180–182 mm) wide and about 1 1/2 inches (37–39 mm) thick.

Throwing the discuss is done from a circular area 8 feet 2 inches (2.5 m) in diameter, three quarters of which is surrounded by a protective cage. The discus is thrown out into a fan-shaped area that opens to an angle of 40°. The judges measure the distance thrown from the edge of the throwing circle to the point of landing.

Hammer Throw

The hammer throw is done from the same throwing area and protective cage as the discus. The cage is even more essential, as the head of the men's hammer is a potentially lethal ball of metal weighing 16 pounds (7.25 kg), swung on the end of a 4-foot (1.215 m) long chain. The women's hammer is 8 pounds 13 ounces (4 kg), and the chain is 3 feet 11 inches (1.2 m) long. To throw, the athlete grips the handle at the end of the chain and makes a complex rotation before releasing the hammer down the field.

The men's hammer-throw record currently stands at 86.86 meters by Yuriy Sedykh of the Soviet Union in 1986, and Russian Tatyana Lysenko set the women's record in 2006, at 77.80 meters.

Shot Put

A shot put is a ball of heavy metal weighing 16 pounds (7.25 kg) in the men's competition and 8 pounds 13 ounces (4 kg) in the women's events. The athlete launches (puts) the shot down a 40° fan from a throwing circle that is 7 feet (2.135 m) in diameter and features a wooden **stopboard** 4 inches (10 cm) high.

High Jump

The high jump involves jumping over a horizontal bar using body power and the momentum of a sprint. The high jump is semicircular in shape, allowing the athlete to make the approach from any angle. They style of the jump itself is up to the athlete; the only rule is that the takeoff of the jump is made from one foot. One technique above all else, however,

An athlete steps into position for a shot put at the University of Pennsylvania's Penn Relays, the nation's oldest and largest track-and-field competition for U.S. high schools and colleges.

TRACK & FIELD

has come to dominate—the "Fosbury Flop," developed by the U.S. athlete Dick Fosbury in the 1960s. It involves the athlete diving over the bar with a backward twist, landing on the crash mat with the shoulders and back. A rectangular crash-mat area 10 by 16 feet (3 x 5 m) provides a safe landing. Using the Fosbury Flop, athletes have achieved amazing heights: the Cuban athlete Javier Sotomayor jumped an incredible 8 feet (2.45 m) in 1993.

Long Jump

The long jump is a distance-jumping competition. The athlete first makes a long sprint of around 130 feet (40 m). At a designated take-off board, the athlete leaps forward into a sand-filled landing about 9 feet (2.75 m) wide and 29 feet (9 m) long. The distance jumped is measured from the take-off board to the first point of impact on the sand (the sand is raked flat after each competitor has jumped to show the impact point clearly). One of the greatest long jumpers of all time was the U.S. athlete Carl Lewis; he holds the men's indoor world record of 28 feet 10 inches (8.79 m).

Pole Vault

The pole vault is athletics' most spectacular event. The poles themselves are made of either fiberglass or carbon fiber, and are chosen by the athlete according to preference or the height of jump. To vault, the athlete runs along a 147-foot (45-m) track, then plants the tip of the pole in a **take-off box** and uses the spring action of the pole to cross the bar. The female Russian gymnast Svetlana Feofanova achieved a height of 15 feet 6 inches (4.75 m) in 2001, while the athlete Sergei Bubka from the Ukraine cleared an incredible 20 feet 2 inches (6.15 m) in 1993.

Triple Jump

The triple jump is essentially a long jump, but the athlete makes a hop and a step before the final jump. After running, the athlete launches from the take-

off board with one leg, and lands on the same leg to make a hop. Then the other leg is used to make a step that launches her forward into the sand-filled landing area. As in a long jump, the distance of the jump is measured from the take-off board to the first impression on the sand. Each stage of the triple jump covers about 33 percent of the total distance.

An athlete at the top of his vault at a pole vault meet in Berlin, Germany.

TRACK & FIELD

TRACK

Sprint

Modern sprinting has three distances: 100 meters (110 yd), 200 meters (220 yd), and 400 meters (440 yd). The 100 meters is run in fixed lanes along a straight track, and today's athletes cover about 10 meters every second. The 200 meters, despite the increased distance, is run at a similar speed; a top international sprinter can reach 25 miles per hours (40 km/h) in the 200 meters and finish within twenty seconds. The biggest tactical difference is that the sprinter has to negotiate a bend during the sprint. The 400 meters involve two bends, and the greatest speed of the race is usually attained during the last straight 100 meters.

Hurdles

There are three categories of hurdles—100 m, 110 m (120 yd), and 400 m—and ten hurdles in each race. The runner is not penalized for knocking down hurdles unless the action is deliberate or the foot goes under the hurdle bar. Today's hurdles are 3 feet 6 inches (106 cm) high for men and 2 feet 9 inches (84 cm) high for women.

Relay

Olympic relay has two distances: 4 x 100 and 4 x 400 meters. The four runners have specific zones in which they must pass over the hollow wooden or plastic baton. These zones are 32 feet (10 m) on either side of the next runner's start line. Apart from the two Olympic distances, other relay distances in non-Olympic competitions include the 3,200 m (3,500 yd) and 6,000 m (6,560 yd).

Middle Distance

Middle-distance track events refer to the 800 m (875 yd) 1,000 m (1,094 yd), and 1,500 m (1,640 yd) distances. In both races, the runners do not have to

Women competing in the women's steeplechase event at the World Athletics Championships in 2007 in Osaka, Japan.

stay in dedicated lanes. The result is a dense group of runners, each using his or her own tactics to attempt victory. Some will attempt to lead from the front the whole way around, while others will hang back in preparation for a final burst of speed.

Steeplechase

Steeplechase is a 3,000-meter (3,280-yd) race featuring hurdles and water jumps. The standard configuration is twenty-eight non-collapsible hurdles, each 3 feet (91 cm) high, and seven water jumps, each preceded by a hurdle. The water jump is 27 inches (70 cm) deep at its deepest point beneath the hurdle, and 12 feet (3.66) long.

TRACK & FIELD

Long-Distance Runs

Excluding marathon and cross-country, the main long-distance track events are the 5,000 meters and the 10,000 meters. These races test stamina and endurance, but they also require tactical running—applying speed at the right times and hanging back occasionally to conserve energy.

Cross-country runners must be able to run across a variety of terrains. Not all courses are as easy as the one shown here!

TRACK-AND-FIELD OVER THE YEARS

Although athletes from the beginning of time have pushed their bodies' limits and strengths to impressive lengths, the athletes of today are without a doubt the most impressive. In all sports, you can see athletes' progression in every way: race times become shorter, length and height become longer and higher, and it seems that each year the bar is raised—literally and figuratively. Today's professional athletes have achieved standards unimaginable at the time of the first Olympics. Take sprinting, for example: at the end of the nineteenth century, Thomas Burke of the United States set a time of 12 seconds for the 100-meter dash. Jump to just over 100 years later in 2009, and Usain Bolt of Jamaica set a new world record of 9.58 seconds for the exact same distance.

These remarkable improvements in performance are, in part, the result of better diet, improved understanding of **physiology**, more advanced training equipment and techniques, and better running shoes. But we cannot take away from the genuine accomplishments of today's athletes.

Cross-Country

Cross-country is run over distances of 2.5, 5, and 7.5 miles (4, 8, and 12 km), although 5 miles is for women only. Cross-country runners handle all types

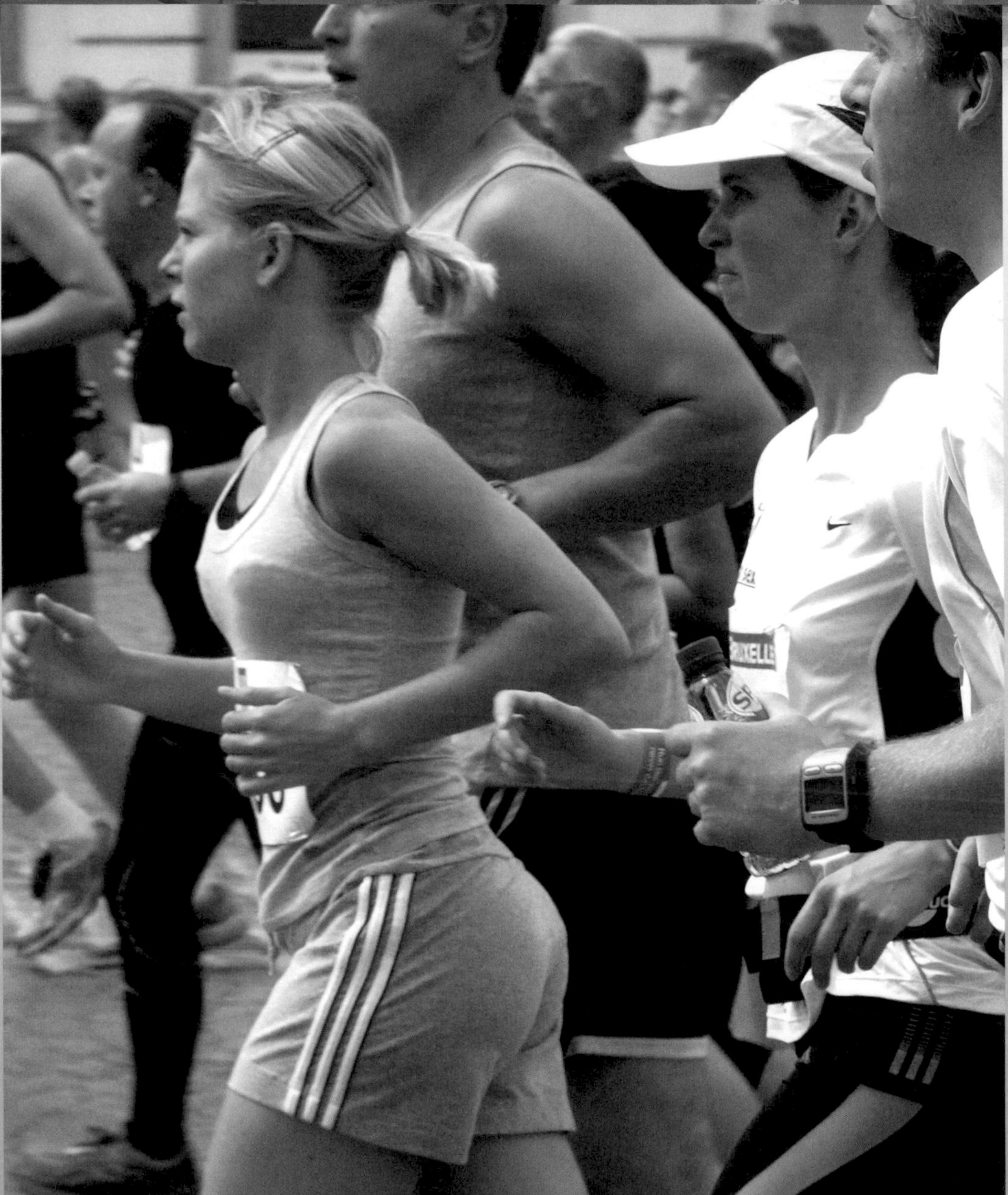

TRACK & FIELD

of terrain and climates, and the body takes a real beating. The runs vary widely in terms of the number of competitors, from fewer than fifty up to many thousands.

Marathon

The marathon was set at a distance of 26 miles (42 km) in 1908. Major marathon events are held in cities throughout the world, including London and Boston, and can draw in more than 25,000 competitors.

Heptathlon and Decathlon

In addition to individual field events, there are two mixed events. These test the athlete through a range of track-and-field challenges. The heptathlon is for women only and consists of seven events: 100-meter hurdles, high jump, shot put, 200-meter race, long jump, javelin, and 800-meter race. The decathlon is a male competition and has ten events: 100-meter sprint, long jump, shot put, high jump, 400-meter run, 100-meter hurdles, discus, javelin, pole vault, and 1,500-meter run. Both events are conducted over two days, with the middle-distance races being the final events.

Thousands of runners may compete in a marathon event like this one in Brussels.

2
Mental Preparation and Safety

Understanding the Words

Visualization *is a technique for improving sports performance by training your mind and imagination.*

A **niche** *is an area or specialization you particularly enjoy or in which you excel.*

Track &FIELD

Ignoring mental preparation is an ideal way for athletes to underperform in competition or practice. The world's best runners and field athletes now often see sports psychologists who can give them the mental edge that they need to succeed in training and competition.

Positive Mental Attitude

There are several factors that distinguish the most successful athletes from those who never achieve their full potential. One of the most important is a positive frame of mind. Professionals are now taught techniques to keep a Positive Mental Attitude (P.M.A.) to improve their performance. How does this work?

First, you must take control of your inner voice, the part of your brain that offers a running commentary on how you feel and think. Say only positive things to yourself when you think about that long jump or spring coming up. Instead of "I'll never win this event," tell yourself, "I can become a top competitor in this event." Instead of "That person is so much better than me," you must think, "I will learn everything I can from them to improve my performance." When you catch yourself focusing on negative thoughts, immediately follow them up with positive contradictions. Repeat this pattern often enough and you will find that P.M.A. becomes a habit—and you will find that competitors or difficult events will not so easily discourage you.

The second element of P.M.A. involves your imagination. Set time aside for mental training, creating positive visual pictures of your performance in running events. The key is to imagine everything, down to the last detail. For example, picture yourself in the 1500-meter pushing out ahead of the pack toward the finish line; hear the noise of the crowd cheering, and feel your shoes hitting the track and the sensation of your deep breathing. Mentally rehearse your technique until it is perfect. Also picture your tactics. In the 1500-meter, a common tactic is to run close behind another competitor to

reduce wind resistance. Then, as you approach the finish line, use the energy you have conserved throughout the race to sprint ahead of the other runner and pass him across the finish line. Practice this tactic in your imagination, and visualize the success it brings you.

The process is known as **visualization**, and its goal is to have a real impact on physical performance. Research has shown that athletes who practice visualization produce better race and event results than those who do not.

Picture yourself in this runner's place, winning the race. Positive visualization has been scientifically proven to help athletes perform better.

The final aspect of P.M.A. includes positive body posture. To see what this means, try this experiment: stand up straight, pull back your shoulders, and lift up your chin. Put a big smile on your face, even if it feels artificial. Go for a brisk ten-minute walk, swinging your arms and filling your lungs with air. Use all your senses to enjoy the world around you. As you do this, you should begin to feel more energetic, lively, and less prone to depression or anxiety. The fact is that our thoughts often follow what our bodies are doing, rather than the other way around. By acting happy and confident, you may actually become happy and confident.

You can use this to help your track-and-field performance. Act like you are a winner. Stand up tall and proud, and imitate the confident athletic behavior of successful professional athletes. Strange as it may seem, acting as if you are going to win your race will actually increase your likelihood of doing so.

Commitment

Many accidents occur among athletes who are mentally distracted while training or competing, or who do not have the discipline to train hard and master techniques. Commitment can help correct both these problems.

If you find that you don't have enough passion for the sport to keep you motivated at practices and competition, it may be that you are simply not interested enough in your sport. If this is the case, it's a good idea to try out another sport or activity to see where your true niche is. However, it may also be that you are simply burned out from too much practice. Boredom kills commitment quickly, so invest in making your sport as interesting as possible. Here are some tips:

- Find out everything you can about your sport—reading books, watching videos, and attending events.

- Talk with professional athletes. Many elite track-and-field competitors have their own websites with blogs or links to email them. Share your problems and thoughts with them, and you might find that they have experienced the same issues in their training.

- Make the effort to travel to watch world-class athletes compete, and be inspired by their performance.

- Organize social outings with other athletes and team members—training should be fun, not just hard work.

- Focus all your energies on winning a particular medal or competition. Although winning is certainly not the most important part of any sport, it will help you become motivated and driven.

- Keep a training journal that records everything about each training session and competition, as well as every bit of progress.

Try thinking of as many ways as possible to feed both your imagination and your passion for the sport.

Fear Control

By preparing fully and working hard on your technique, you will go a long way toward mastering another problem—fear. Athletes can be afraid of many things: failure, injury, embarrassment, or letting the team down. Fear is a dangerous feeling to take into track-and-field events. Fear can take away your ability to concentrate and to move with confidence. In events such as the pole vault, this can be lethal. When the vaulter is ascending heights of up to 52 feet 6 inches (16 m) on the pole, there is a point that she is upside down and facing away from the landing mat; all she can see is the ground beneath

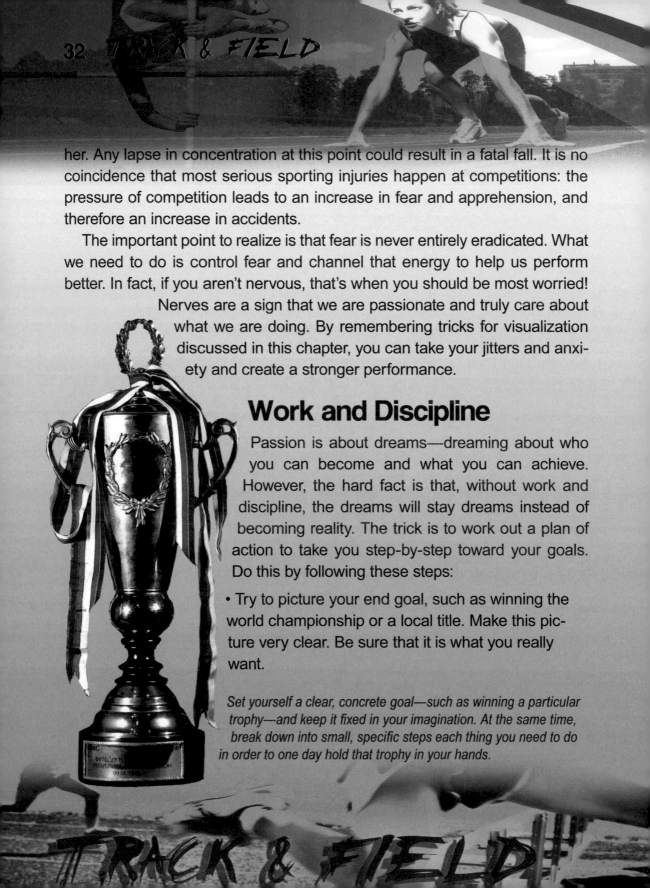

her. Any lapse in concentration at this point could result in a fatal fall. It is no coincidence that most serious sporting injuries happen at competitions: the pressure of competition leads to an increase in fear and apprehension, and therefore an increase in accidents.

The important point to realize is that fear is never entirely eradicated. What we need to do is control fear and channel that energy to help us perform better. In fact, if you aren't nervous, that's when you should be most worried!

Nerves are a sign that we are passionate and truly care about what we are doing. By remembering tricks for visualization discussed in this chapter, you can take your jitters and anxiety and create a stronger performance.

Work and Discipline

Passion is about dreams—dreaming about who you can become and what you can achieve. However, the hard fact is that, without work and discipline, the dreams will stay dreams instead of becoming reality. The trick is to work out a plan of action to take you step-by-step toward your goals. Do this by following these steps:

• Try to picture your end goal, such as winning the world championship or a local title. Make this picture very clear. Be sure that it is what you really want.

Set yourself a clear, concrete goal—such as winning a particular trophy—and keep it fixed in your imagination. At the same time, break down into small, specific steps each thing you need to do in order to one day hold that trophy in your hands.

- Working backward through time, think of every step you need to take to reach that final goal. For example, to win a regional title, you must first be selected for the team. To be selected, you must pass the team tryouts on a particular date. To pass the team tryouts, you must improve your qualifying performance in the long jump. Work backward in this way until you are at the present.

- What you have now is a breakdown of your major goals into small, manageable steps. Look at the first step on your list. Devote all your resources to achieving this goal. The important point is that for each step, you develop an action plan. In short, an action plan is what you will actually do to make the step happen. Work out the practical needs and then, most important, start them now. Beware of phrases like "I'll start this tomorrow." Once you have made the decision to achieve something, start working toward it today.

- Draw up an action plan for your training routine. At the beginning of each week, write down in a diary when you will train, what you will work on, and what you hope to achieve by the end of each session. Planning and preparation are what separates winners from other competitors. Keep a training log of everything that happened during a particular training session or competition. The advantage of a well-kept training log is that you can see exactly what you need to work on. It can also reveal why you are suffering from certain injuries. You may notice, for example, that you have been suffering from pain only since you started attempting a new technique in shot put. This will indicate that you need to alter your technique or strengthen your shoulder muscles.

Coaching Relationship

A good coach is as essential in track-and-field as in any other sport. There are literally thousands of track-and-field coaches in the United States. Picking out the professionals from the less qualified can be difficult, but remember, a good coach will:

- Explain techniques clearly and simply.
- Have approved coaching qualifications from a governing body such as USATF.
- Make you feel good about yourself and give you plenty of positive feedback.

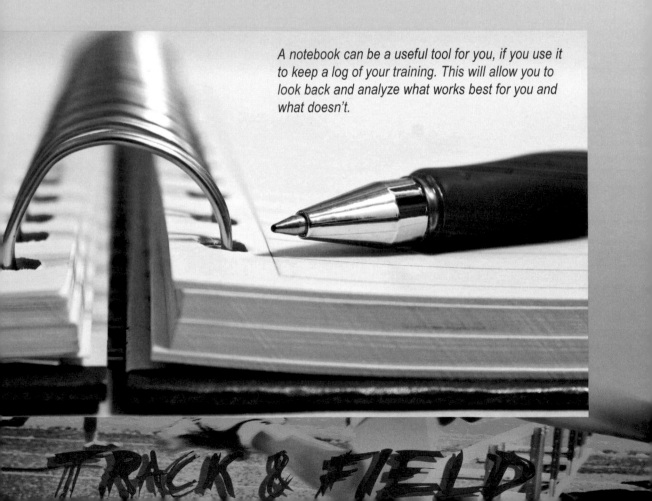

A notebook can be a useful tool for you, if you use it to keep a log of your training. This will allow you to look back and analyze what works best for you and what doesn't.

- Give you days off to rest your body and mind.

- Have a clear structure and objective to every training session.

- Understand the physiology of sports, and know how to handle injuries.

- Make time for extra training in preparation for competitions.

Competitions

Your mental training matters more than ever in competitions. Many fine athletes have been defeated in races because a lack of confidence spoils their physical ability. Competitions are undoubtedly nerve-wracking events, but there are several things you can do to help you harness your nervousness so that instead of weakening your body, it makes you run faster.

- Pack up everything you need for the race before you go to bed. This means you will probably sleep better and also have a more restful morning on the day of the race.

- Eat properly throughout the day. Do not eat large, meaty meals because these will make you feel sluggish and lacking in energy, particularly if your race is in the afternoon, following lunch. Also, make sure you have a good, healthy breakfast: cereal, toast, orange juice, and fruit. Breakfast is the most important meal of the day because your brain needs it for energy throughout the morning.

- Warm up properly once you get to the place where the race or event is being held. Not only will this loosen up your body and prepare it for the race, but it will also help you focus your mind on what you need to do.

- Psych yourself up. Focus one hundred percent on the race ahead of you. Find a place by yourself, where you can shut out other concerns and concentrate on the techniques needed to win. If you find it helps,

TRACK & FIELD

play your favorite music on your iPod or MP3 player. Also, do not be intimidated by other competitors. Concentrate solely on getting from the starting line to the finish line in the fastest possible time, and forget about others' behavior.

- Learn from your losses. Defeats are not easy to accept, but you must learn to cope with them if you are going to improve. Steve Scott, the U.S. record holder in the 1-mile run, gives the following advice for coping with disappointment: "I give myself an hour, two hours tops, to be upset or angry about a bad race. I think about what went wrong and why it might have gone wrong, but I don't beat myself up about it." Like Steve, do not allow yourself to feel depressed or over think a bad performance. Quickly concentrate on why the race was a problem, and write down in your training log anything that occurs to you. Return to your training with renewed enthusiasm, determined to conquer your problems and smash your times in the next race in which you compete.

Checking Your Progress

A major part of your mental training should be keeping track of your progress. Keep an account of your times, competition performance, and medals to help you see how far you have come, and also to identify those areas which need more work. The best way of keeping track is through a training log. The training log is a notebook or computer database for recording day-to-day details about your athletic training. The following are the types of information you want to include in each entry:

- date
- weather

- type of workout or run

- type of footwear worn

- times or measurements achieved

- warm-up and cool-down techniques used

- special training techniques

- notes about performance or injuries

3
Physical Preparation

Understanding the Words

Tendons are tough bands of connective tissue that connect muscles to bones.

Fast twitch muscle fibers are naturally better at generating short bursts of strength or speed than slow muscles; they also become tired more quickly.

Flexors are skeletal muscles that, when they contract, bend joints and decrease the angle between limbs. Examples of this are the knees or elbows. This action is also referred to as flexion.

The **gluteus maximus** muscle forms the majority of the buttocks and extends into the upper leg muscles. It is the largest muscle in the human body, and is commonly referred to as the "glutes."

Any exercise in which muscles are repeatedly and rapidly stretched and then contracted is termed a **plyometrics** exercise; the aim is to improve muscle power.

Muscle fibers are made of myofibrils, which are strands of proteins, and are responsible for the muscles' ability to bend, or contract.

Free weights are weight-training equipment that is made up of weights, such as dumbbells, that are placed on a bar when not in use.

Weight machines come in a variety of types and provide various resistance exercises used in weight training.

A **set** is a complete group of repetitions.

Understanding the Words

continued

The **power phase** in weight training is the phase where the weight is lifted, pulled, or pushed; it is the period where the most energy is exerted.

Antagonistic pairs are sets of muscles that work together. These muscles can contract and relax but cannot push or stretch without the help of the other part of its set.

The **quadriceps** is the large four-part muscle on the front of each thigh, used to extend the leg.

Hamstrings are the groups of three muscles located on the back of the thighs.

Dead lift exercise is the lifting of weights from a standing position without using any support equipment, such as a bench.

Aerobic exercise is any exercise that demands increased oxygen and forces up the heart and breathing rate.

Cross training is the combination of several sports in one training program to improve fitness.

Cardiovascular exercise is any exercise that improves the health and function of the heart and lungs.

Preventing injury in sports requires increased strength and flexibility in the vulnerable muscles, **tendons**, and ligaments surrounding the joints. The muscles and joints most at risk are those that endure repeated stress and heavy loads during exercise, or those that are exposed to sudden, explosive movements.

For example, triple jumpers are susceptible to overuse injuries in the muscles and tendons that join the thighbone to the hip joint. By contrast, discus and javelin competitors are in danger of rupturing their back muscles from the twisting and hurling actions in their events.

Warm-Up and Conditioning Drills

The first and foremost important part of safety in track-and-field is warming up. Jumping right into an event is not smart, and more often than not, it will result in a sprained, torn, or otherwise injured body part. As tedious as it may seem, always take the proper time to warm up before practice or an event or race. Here are a variety of warm-up exercises that will get your blood pumping and muscles loosened no matter what the event.

BACKWARD EXTENSION

Find a clear, open space with no obstacles, and begin running backward, extending your legs as far as they will reach. The goal is to get as much backward extension as possible to help develop **fast twitch** muscles, **hamstrings**, quads, and hip flexors.

JUMP SKIPS FOR HEIGHT

Skip on the right foot and at the same time, drive your left knee up as high as it will go. Then repeat with the left foot skipping and the right knee driving up. The arms are very important in this drill, as they must be constantly pumping up and down. Whichever foot is skipping on the ground, that same arm must be driving up as well.

Keep the arm at a 90-degree angle from the elbows, hands pointed straight ahead, back and shoulders slightly arched. The goal is to obtain as much height as possible; this drill will develop proper form as you compete in an event.

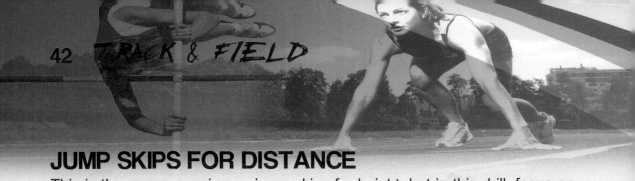

JUMP SKIPS FOR DISTANCE

This is the same exercise as jump skips for height, but in this drill, focus on getting as far down the track as you can while extending the leg. Push off with the calf muscles and make sure your arms are driving up at a constant pace.

KARAOKE

Standing up straight, look to the right over your shoulder and put your hands out to the side for balance. Moving quickly but under control, cross your left leg over your right leg. Then, stride with your right leg toward the direction you are moving, and cross your left leg behind your right one, swiveling your hips

The land in the sand pit after a long jump can put stress on your hips and back.

as you move sideways. Continue this pattern quickly, crossing and uncrossing your legs as fast as you can. This exercise will increase your speed and reaction time.

MAXIMUMS

This drill is a great way to warm up, as well as improve your running form. Start by running a 50-yard distance at about 50 percent (100 percent being a sprint as fast as you can possibly go.) Focus on keeping proper running form, drive the arms, relax the hands and jaw, and make sure your knees are driving up high and far so you get as long a stride as possible. Stop at 50 yards, walk back, and rest for one minute.

Run the same 50 yards again, but increasing to 60 percent effort, then 70 percent, 80 percent, 90 percent, and finally 100 percent at a full sprint. At each speed, be sure to maintain proper form.

Demands on the Body

Field events and running events place different demands on the human body. Athletes must have well-rounded physiques that are strong and flexible at every level. However, they must also condition the parts of the body that are put under the most stress by their chosen events.

- running—hamstrings, **quadriceps**, ankles, foot **flexors**, and the **gluteus maximus**
- discus—shoulders, arms, lower back, hips, knees
- javelin—shoulders, elbows, groin, upper and lower back, hips
- hammer—shoulders, elbows, back, abdominals, hips, knees
- shot put—shoulders, arms, abdominals, back, and legs
- high jump—spine, ankles, knees, hips

TRACK & FIELD

- pole vault—shoulders, abdominals, back

- long jump—ankles, knees, hips, back

- triple jump—ankles, knees, hips, back

Athletes must give special attention to preparing the muscle groups and joints that are most worked by their sport.

Importance of Flexibility

Flexibility, the systematic lengthening of muscles, is one of the most important aspects of not just track-and-field, but any sport. A flexible athlete has many advantages that a non-flexible athlete does not: a flexible muscle is far less likely to sustain injury under stress because it has a greater range of movement. Also, a flexible runner will be faster than one who is not flexible; she will be able to make longer strides with each step.

Regardless of the type of stretches, here are some general rules to follow:

- Stop immediately if you feel any sudden pains or growing burning sensations. Also, stop if you feel nauseated, faint, or ill in any way.

- Keep breathing deeply through any stretch—your muscles need a constant supply of oxygen to get the most out of the stretch.

- Make sure that you stretch after you have completed a workout. The muscles, which will be tired and sore from being overworked, recover more quickly if they are stretched as the body is cooling down. Stretching prevents the muscles from tightening up and becoming stiff.

STRETCHES FOR TRACK-AND-FIELD EVENTS

The following stretches are excellent for loosening up the hips, waist, and back—all areas that are prone to injury.

Hip/Groin Stretch

- Stand with your legs in an "A"-shape about two shoulder-widths apart.
- Bend forward from the waist, and take your body weight on your hands.
- Slowly sink your hips downward, inching your legs wider and wider apart. Continue breathing deeply.
- When you are as far down as your body will allow, hold the position for five to ten seconds and let your body relax. You may then be able to go down a bit farther.

Stretching is an important part of every runner's routine.

TRACK & FIELD

• When you have reached your maximum stretch, come out of it by walking your feet inward (while maintaining your weight on your hands) until you are able to stand up.

Waist and Back Stretch

• Stand upright, with your feet shoulder-width apart.

• Bend straight forward from the waist and lower your torso as far as it will go, keeping your back straight.

• Hold the legs and gently pull on them to go down farther. Hold the stretch for ten seconds, then pull your body upright again.

• Put your hands against your lower back and stretch your body backward, looking up at the ceiling as you do. Do not bend your head too far, as this could lead to a neck strain. Hold for ten seconds.

STRETCHES FOR RUNNERS

Ankle Stretch

Sitting down, put the left ankle on top of the right knee. Hold the raised ankle with your left hand, and take hold of the toes and the ball of the foot with your right hand. Using your right hand, circle the foot around in one direction in large circles. Repeat about ten times, then reverse and repeat with the other foot.

Achilles Tendon Stretch

Lie on your back with both knees bent and feet flat on the floor. Straighten one leg up into the air and hold it with both hands on the calf muscle. Pull your leg gently toward your face until it is at its maximum stretch. Then flex the raised foot slowly backward and forward about ten times, working the Achilles tendon.

Lower Leg Stretch

Sit on the floor with both legs straight out in front of you. Draw one leg in so that the sole of the foot sits against the inner thigh of the opposite leg. Sit up straight and breathe in deeply, then exhale slowly and bend forward from the hips and waist over the extended leg until you can grip your foot. Slowly pull on the toes so that the heel lifts slightly off the floor. You should feel a deep stretch along the back of the leg and knee. Lower the heel to the floor and sit up slowly. Then reverse legs and repeat the exercise.

Quadriceps Stretch

Stand up straight, resting one hand against a wall for stability. Lift your leg behind you and grasp the top of the foot with your left hand, then pull the heel up toward your buttocks. You should feel the stretch along the front of the thigh and knee. Hold the position for about thirty seconds, then let go of the foot and return it to the floor. Repeat with your right leg.

Training

There are several aspects of training for track-and-field that contribute to your performance. Not only must you practice your specific event, but it is also important to focus on separate areas and strengths of the body individually. For both field and running events, **plyometric** training is essential, as is weight training. For events that take place over a longer period of time, such as middle-distance running, endurance is extremely important.

PLYOMETRICS

Plyometric training is a vital part of training in any sport that involves sudden, explosive movements, so it is particularly important to field and sprinting events. A relatively modern branch of sports training, it aims to condition the muscles to make contraction movements in the short amount of time.

Plyometric exercises have to be specifically tailored to the individual sport or event in order to be the most effective. For example, if you are a javelin or discus thrower, focus on upper-body plyometrics; if you do the long jump, lower-body plyometrics will help you the most.

Specific plyometric exercises concentrate on short, vigorous movements followed instantly by a relaxation phase. They are now an essential part of any field athlete's training regime because they are extremely useful in reducing injuries. But always be sure to learn these exercises under the supervision of a qualified coach or personal training. There are many plyometrics exercises, so your coach should be able to provide you with a practice routine specific to your event(s). Here are two basic exercises to demonstrate.

Upper Body

The athlete lies on the floor with a partner standing over him. The partner drops a medicine ball from a height at the chest of the athlete. The athlete catches the ball and immediately throws it back. This exercise trains the rapid expansion and contraction of the arms that is vital for throwing events.

Lower Body

The athlete jumps from the ground onto a box or step between 12 and 31 inches (30–80 cm) high, then immediately jumps back off. This should be practiced carefully, beginning with a lower height and working upward. It conditions the legs for spring starts and for jumping events.

STRENGTH TRAINING

Strength training, or resistance exercises, are those that use the muscles to lift, pull, or push weight. They create stronger and larger muscles by producing more and tougher **muscle fibers** in order to cope with the increasing weight demands.

The best form of body-strengthening exercise is weight training. Weight training uses either **free weights** or **weight machines** to strengthen muscles.

However it carries real risk of injury if done incorrectly, especially for athletes who are under eighteen years old. Always get professional training first from your coach or other instructor before trying anything on your own. Follow these key rules for safe and effective results:

- When learning any new technique, practice it first without any weight at all until you can demonstrate perfect technique to an instructor. Once you have the right technique, add only light weights that you can handle easily.

- Add further weights in 1- to 3-pound (0.5-1.5 kg) increments, and perform one to three sets at the new weight. Once you can demonstrate perfect technique again at the new weight, more weight can continue to be added.

- Do not train more than three times a week, in thirty-minute sessions.

- Do all exercises slowly, with total control and concentration. It should take three full seconds to perform the **power phase** of the exercise, and three full seconds to relax the weight.

Plyometric exercises often make use of medicine balls to build muscle strength.

TRACK & FIELD

- Keep breathing deeply throughout the power phase, and during the relaxation phase.

- Always warm up thoroughly before doing weights. Cold muscles are susceptible to injury.

- Be systematic about how you develop your body. Always develop your muscles in **antagonistic pairs**. For example, if you develop the bicep on the inside of the arm, you develop the triceps on the outside of the arm equally. This concept also applies to the back and abdominals, and the quadriceps and hamstrings.

- If you are under eighteen, do not attempt heavy **dead lift** exercises. These put too much strain on the developing physique.

Weight training helps build the upper-body strength necessary for many field events.

There are a nearly infinite number of weight training exercises, especially event-specific ones that focus on a certain muscle or muscle group. To get the best results, work one-on-one with your coach or personal trainer, who can help you develop a routine tailored to your event.

ENDURANCE

Endurance is a type of **aerobic** training in which the body requires increased amounts of oxygen in order to perform. The body gets this oxygen by raising the heart and breathing rates, then sustaining both at the increased level. Aerobic exercise is vital for injury prevention because it strengthens the heart muscles and lungs to cope with strenuous exercise. By gaining endurance, you will be able to run or perform for a longer period of time without becoming exhausted and out of breath. This will not only increase your performance times, but also your health.

Fortunately, being a track-and-field athlete means that you probably get all the aerobic exercise you need from running. Do not, however, rely upon running alone. The best aerobic fitness comes from **cross training**, which entails mixing different aerobic events in your training schedule. Use two or three different types of aerobic training to ensure that your **cardiovascular** system is strong, and also to develop different muscle groups. An excellent combination would be running, swimming, and cycling: running and cycling improve lower limb flexibility and strength, while swimming enhances the shoulders, arms, back, and abdominals. One caution: even if you are extremely fit in one sport, do not jump into a different sport at the same speed. Different sports have different muscular demands, so give your body time to adjust to the new exercise. Also, make sure that you have at least two days a week of compete rest. Any less than that and you run a risk of injury through overtraining because your muscles will not have time to recover or strengthen.

Basketball is a great way to maintain aerobic fitness.

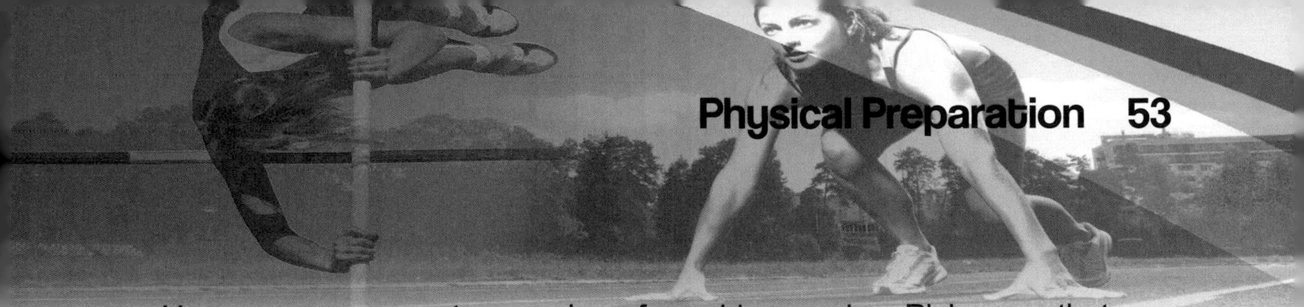

Here are some great examples of aerobic exercise. Pick ones that you most enjoy, so training can be more enjoyable, rather than an obligation.

• jumping rope

• playing basketball

• roller skating or rollerblading

• dancing

• kayaking

• ice skating

TRACK & FIELD

4
Common Injuries, Treatment, & Recovery

Understanding the Words

P.R.I.C.E. *is an acronym for the common method for treating non-serious sprains and strains: Protection, Rest, Ice, Compression, and Elevation.*

R.O.M. *is the abbreviation for Range of Motion, which refers to exercises designed to reintroduce flexibility into an injured joint or muscle.*

The **rotator cuff** *is a group of muscles that hold the shoulder joint in place, enabling the rotational movement of each arm.*

The **biceps** *muscles are the large muscles on the inside of the upper arm, which flex the arm and forearm.*

The **triceps** *are the muscles on the back of the upper arm.*

Anti-inflammatories *are any medications that reduce swelling.*

G-forces *are caused by a combination of gravity and acceleration. They create a strong sense of being pushed back that is generated by rapid acceleration; pilots experience this when they are taking off.*

Physical therapy *is using physical techniques, like massage and stretching, to treat an illness or injury. It is an alternative to using medicines or surgery.*

track
&FIELD

Understanding the Words

continued

The **tibia** is the large bone between the knee and the ankle.

The **femur** is another word for the thighbone.

Ligaments are short bands of tough body tissue that connect bones or hold joints together.

Tendons are cords of body tissue that connect muscles to bones.

Sports injuries usually happen suddenly through an accident or strain, or gradually through wear and tear over a long period of time. It is important to know not only how to treat these injuries once they occur, but how to prevent them from happening in the first place. In a sport like track-and-field where each event is specialized, specific areas of the body need special attention.

P.R.I.C.E.

The good news about injuries is that many do not need professional treatment—mainly non-serious sprains and strains—and these may be treated in three stages. The first of these stages can be easily remembered by using the acronym **P.R.I.C.E.**, which stands for protection, rest, ice, compression, and elevation.

PROTECTION

As soon as you feel an injury or any unexplained pain, you need to stop playing and get off the court as quickly as possible. Move to a place or position where you can take pressure off the injury.

REST

Give the injured area complete rest for at least a week. Restrict other activities and sports that affect the injury to a minimum, including everyday walking.

ICE

Reduce any swelling around the injury by applying ice packs about two or three times a day, for no longer than twenty minutes each time. If there is no swelling, however, you may find it more helpful to apply heat treatments after the first few days. Heat-generating ointments are available from sports stores and drug stores, and are useful for reducing pain caused by muscle strains. Do not use heat treatments on swelling or swollen areas.

COMPRESSION

Wrap the injury firmly in a bandage or athletic tape. Even better, use a professional compression bandage. The pressure around the injury reduces swelling, and also protects the joint or muscle against further damage.

ELEVATION

Elevate an injured limb on a surface—a chair or table, for example—that is well padded with cushions. If the leg is injured, try to raise it higher than the hips. Elevation reduces the amount of blood flowing into a limb and helps reduce swelling.

R.O.M. Exercises

Following the P.R.I.C.E. procedure alone may enable you to return to training after about a week and is ideal for sprained ankles, a common running injury. If, however, the injured muscle or joint is pain-free but stiff or weak after the treatment, two more procedures may be tried. First is range-of-motion (R.O.M.) exercises. These are light stretching and flexibility exercises, meant

A runner treats shin splints by wrapping her leg in ice after an 8-kilometer run.

to restore the full range of movement to the joint or limb. The stretches are gentle, but should explore movement in every direction that was possible before the accident. The goal is to achieve full mobility without any stiffness or pain.

Once you have full, pain-free R.O.M., you need to strengthen the injured joint or muscle. Light weight training is a good way to achieve this. Barbell squats, leg extensions, leg presses, leg curls, and hip adduction are excellent rehabilitation exercises for the lower limbs (ask your coach or local gym for details). Do not load the bar or weight machine with heavy weights. Practice first lifting weights of only 1 to 2 pounds (0.501 kg) until you can perform the technique perfectly for at least eight repetitions without struggling. Add more weight in 1- to 3-pound (0.5-1.5 kg) increments. Such gentle weight training over a period of about seven days should get your injured joint or muscle back into condition.

Stop exercising if the pain returns at any stage during rehabilitation, or if you experience any burning sensations in the joint or muscle. Remember, too, that self-treatment is an option only for simple and identifiable injuries. If you are not sure what is wrong or are experiencing significant pain consult a doctor immediately.

Symptoms of Overuse Injuries

Overuse injuries present with both mental and physical symptoms.

MENTAL SYMPTOMS

- unusual tiredness or fatigue
- feeling very emotional, particularly depressed, anxious, or stressed

- feelings of guilt about any time you are not training

- lack of appetite

- an inability to sleep at night

PHYSICAL SYMPTOMS

- muscle soreness and cramps

- stiff, painful, or unstable joints

- problems getting certain parts of the body comfortable in bed at night

- tension headaches

- painful tendons

- pain that shows no improvement after three days

Event-Specific Injuries

Because the sport of track-and-field can vary so much from event to event, you cannot always take training, warm-up, or injury-related advice from a teammate, especially if he competes in the long jump and you throw shot put. The descriptions listed here will show you what you need to watch out for during training and competition, and how to best deal with injuries if they do occur. Again, always be sure to consult with your coach or trainer, because he will ultimately know what is best for your situation.

THROWING INJURIES

Throwing injuries mainly affect the upper limbs. Discus throwing, shot put, javelin, and hammer throw all have different actions, but all put immense strain on the shoulder's **rotator cuff**, the **biceps** and **triceps** in the arms, and the elbow. The elbow and shoulder often suffer the most injuries.

The rotator cuff in the shoulder is the group of muscles and tendons that attach the upper-arm bone (the humerus) to the shoulder joint and also enable the arm's rotational movement. The rotator cuff allows for more than 75 percent of all shoulder injuries in sports. During throwing events, it has to cope with the cocking of the arm as it gets ready to throw, the sudden acceleration of the arm as the object is thrown, and the equally sudden stopping of the arm at the end of the throw. When these actions are repeated over and over again, muscles in the rotator cuff can be torn or ruptured.

Athletes throwing shot puts and hammers are particularly prone to rotator cuff injuries because of the weight of the object being thrown.

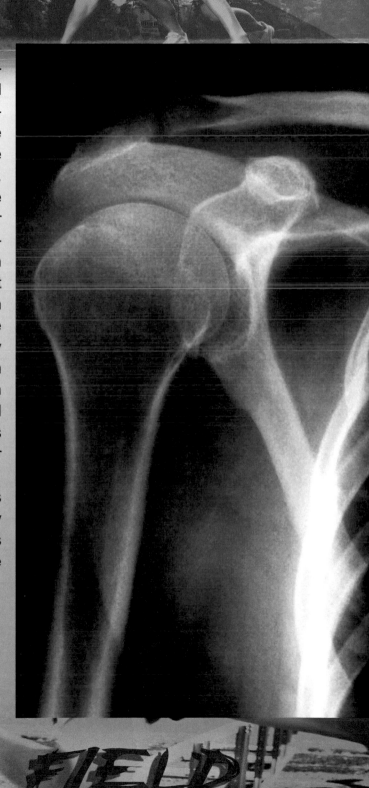

Rotator cuff injuries are common in track events like discus and javelin throwing.

Symptoms of a damaged rotator cuff include:

• intense pain in the shoulder, which may radiate down the upper arm.

• an increase in pain when the arm is rotated or when attempting to lift objects.

• a concentration of pain at night in bed, and the inability to make yourself comfortable because of the shoulder pain.

• limited movement of the arm.

• an inflamed shoulder joint.

• weakness in the movement of the arm at some points.

• clicking and popping sensations in the shoulder during movement.

ROTATOR CUFF INJURIES

Rehabilitating a torn rotator cuff begins with total rest from training. Reduce arm activity to a minimum until the pain in the shoulder has subsided, which may take about a week. Use the P.R.I.C.E. procedure, also, under the guidance of a doctor or pharmacist, use **anti-inflammatories** to bring pain and swelling under control.

R.O.M. exercises can be as simple as moving the arm gently through its full range of movement. To strengthen the shoulder, try upper-arm weight training exercises using light 1-pound (500-g) dumbbells. Vary the exercises frequently to strengthen all parts of the rotator cuff. The following are two typical exercises:

• Hold the dumbbell to the side of the body, then raise your arm straight out to the side until it is at shoulder length. The thumb should be pointing downward. Hold for three seconds, then gently lower. Repeat two more times.

After a rotator cuff injury, exercise can help rebuild strength in the shoulder.

- Hold the dumbbell to the side of the body, then swing it forward with a straight arm until your arm reaches a vertical position with the dumbbell above your head. Hold for three seconds, then gently lower. Repeat.

TRACK & FIELD

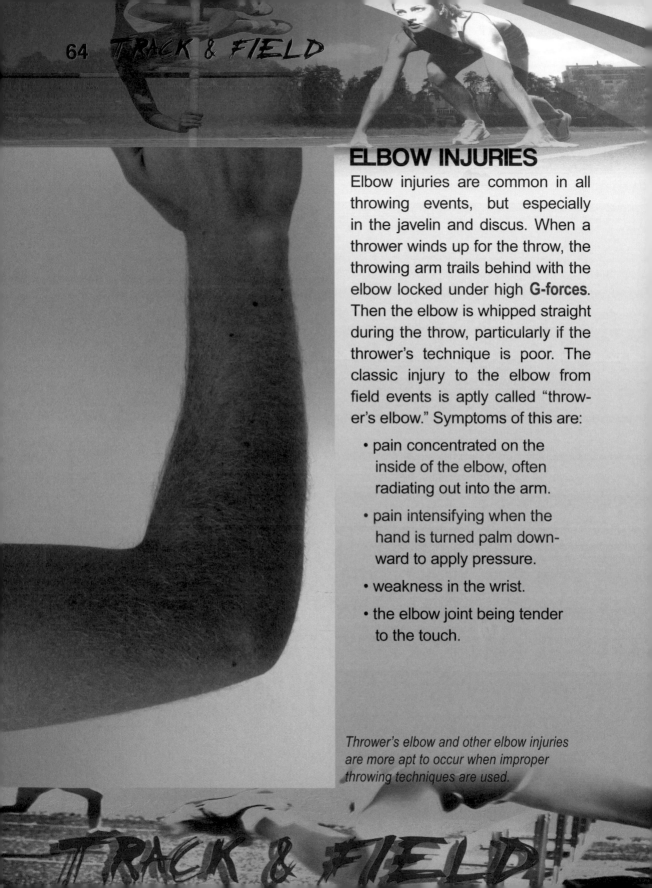

ELBOW INJURIES

Elbow injuries are common in all throwing events, but especially in the javelin and discus. When a thrower winds up for the throw, the throwing arm trails behind with the elbow locked under high **G-forces**. Then the elbow is whipped straight during the throw, particularly if the thrower's technique is poor. The classic injury to the elbow from field events is aptly called "thrower's elbow." Symptoms of this are:

- pain concentrated on the inside of the elbow, often radiating out into the arm.

- pain intensifying when the hand is turned palm downward to apply pressure.

- weakness in the wrist.

- the elbow joint being tender to the touch.

Thrower's elbow and other elbow injuries are more apt to occur when improper throwing techniques are used.

Thrower's elbow and many other non-severe elbow injuries, can be treated with P.R.I.C.E., R.O.M., and strengthening exercises. Start the R.O.M. exercises as soon as possible. The elbow has a tendency to stiffen up dramatically after injury, and can degenerate further if the joint is not loosened. Elbow R.O.M. exercises are simple and can be done anywhere. Try this easy exercise:

- Stand up straight with the arm by your side, palm facing up.
- Slowly bend your elbow as far as possible, drawing your hand up to your shoulder. Hold for three seconds, then lower slowly.
- Repeat ten times.

To strengthen the elbow, perform the same exercise using a light dumbbell.

RUNNING AND JUMPING INJURIES

The main body parts affected by jumping and running are the ankles, knees, hamstrings, and spine. Ankles and knees suffer mainly from sudden thrusting forces as the athlete begins a sprint, and for jumpers, when she pushes off violently for a jump. In the case of long jumpers and triple jumpers, the lower limbs also have to withstand impact in the sand pit.

Ankle and knee joints can develop a range of problems from jumping activities, including torn muscles, **tendons**, and **ligaments**. The symptoms of these injuries include reduced mobility, pain, difficulty in putting pressure on the joint, limping, and general discomfort. P.R.I.C.E. will control the swelling and pain of the injury. Like the elbow, the ankle and knee joints benefit from early R.O.M., but keep this light to prevent overworking the already damaged joint.

- For the knee, try sitting on a high chair or table, moving the lower leg backward and forward through its full range of movement to reintroduce mobility. This will also serve to strengthen the knee joint.

TRACK & FIELD

- For the ankle, simply circle the foot in both directions and pull gently backward and forward to release its movement.

- An additional ankle-strengthening exercise is to slowly raise yourself up on tiptoe and hold for five seconds, then lower yourself back down.

- Strengthening the knee and ankle can be done by walking. Walk on flat surfaces only, slowly building up to inclines for increased strengthening. Be particularly careful when walking down hills and steps. Many knee and ankle injuries are made worse by downward movement, so rest your legs first on a short incline before attempting an entire hillside.

Something as simple as rising up and down on your tiptoes will help strengthen your ankles.

As with all the injuries described, stop rehabilitation exercises immediately if you have any sudden or growing pains.

HAMSTRING INJURIES

The hamstrings are commonly damaged in running and jumping events. They are a group of three muscles set at the back of each thigh that flex the knee joint. They are usually damaged in sprinting, especially during explosive starts from the blocks and fast accelerations. The injured person may feel a distinctive popping sensation at the moment of rupture, following by pain at the back of the thigh and limited mobility in the knee. Sometimes, there may be swelling and even bruising behind the knee.

Most hamstring injuries are fully treatable by following the P.R.I.C.E., R.O.M., and strengthening procedures. For the R.O.M. stage, use the following exercise:

Sit on the edge of a table, with one leg over the edge of the table and the other running straight along the side. Keeping the back straight, bend forward from the waist over the outstretched leg until you feel a stretch in the back of the thigh and hamstring. Hold for fifteen seconds, then release. Repeat the sequence five times. Repeat the exercises for the other leg.

ACHILLES TENDON INJURIES

The Achilles tendon is the prominent tendon at the back of the heel, which joins the heel to the muscles of the lower leg. Runners tend to injure it in two ways. First is Achilles tendonitis, where the Achilles tendon suffers from gradual wear and tear, producing a steady buildup of pain and stiffness at the back of the heel. Running up hills and wearing running shoes with very stiff soles or very deep, soft heels are major causes of Achilles tendonitis because these can lead to excessive stretching of the tendon.

More serious than tendonitis is a complete rupture. The cause of a ruptured Achilles tendon may be a twisted ankle, but it is more commonly associated with excessive stretching exercises. A ruptured tendon will be agonizing, and the ankle will be almost immobile, leaving you in no doubt that you must consult a doctor. Treating Achilles tendonitis may be a simple matter of reducing your training commitments. Avoid long-distance runs and strenuous hills, and make sure you have at least three days each week with no exercise. Apply ice packs to reduce pain and swelling. During rehabilitation, it is best to avoid putting the Achilles tendon through stretching exercises. Instead, do gentle circling of the foot and ankle. Strengthen the tendon by gradually returning to running.

A ruptured tendon is usually treated by surgery, after which you may be in a cast for twelve weeks and possibly have **physical**

A knee brace can help keep the joint stable while it heals after an injury.

therapy for up to one year. You cannot treat a ruptured tendon yourself, and you should always follow the guidance of a qualified doctor.

KNEE INJURIES

The knee is a complicated joint that joins the **tibia** bone of the lower leg and the **femur** bone of the thigh, and it includes many working parts. The symptoms of knee damage in runners usually include:

- pain down the side or front of the knee. Depending on the condition, the pain often worsens with exercise, particularly when running or walking down hills.

- stiffness in the joint.

- pain following periods of sitting with the knees bent.

The P.R.I.C.E., R.O.M., and strengthening sequences of treatment usually suffice to treat a minor knee injury. You may benefit, however, from reducing the P.R.I.C.E. period or even skipping it altogether. Studies in knee rehabilitation have found that an injured knee joint tends to benefit from movement and light exercise. Sitting on a high chair or table, practice moving the lower leg backward and forward through its full range of movement to reintroduce mobility and strength. For additional support, you can put a physical therapy ball under the foot to take pressure off the knee. Further strengthening is available through lower-limb weight-training exercises, but only if you experience no significant pain. Try the exercises without weights before proceeding.

Return to running gently. For the first few weeks, try to avoid running continuously around track bends—these put the knee under more pressure. Consult a doctor if the pain in the knee increases or knee flexibility decreases at any time during rehabilitation. Also consult a doctor if the joint feels unstable or its movement is rough.

SHIN SPLINTS

"Shin splints" is a non-technical name for medial tibial stress syndrome. It refers to pain that occurs in the front or side of the shin, caused by injury to the bone, muscles, or ligaments in the area as a result of hard sporting activity. Shin splints are a classic runner's injury. They tend to happen to athletes who are overtraining or running on hard tracks or other hard surfaces. In fact, if you suddenly change running surfaces—as in moving from cross-country to track—increase your time on the new surface gradually in order to reduce the risk of shin splints.

The symptoms of shin splints include:

- pain in the shin area that grows worse with activity and lets up with rest.

- some swelling over the shin area.

- pain in the shin when the foot is flexed.

Virtually the only treatment for shin splints is rest. Stop training immediately and let the injury heal naturally, which could take up to four months in severe cases. Swimming and cycling are the best exercises to keep you fit during rehabilitation. Both of these sports limit the amount of pressure on the injury while enabling you to keep the muscles in shape. Ease back into training with short, undemanding runs. If the pain returns, rest for longer or go to a doctor.

HIP INJURIES

Like knee injuries, hip injuries are of many different causes and types. Women seem to be slightly more prone to hip injuries than men, but all runners may experience painful or clicking hips from time to time. The symptoms depend on the type of injury. Ruptured muscles or tendons make themselves know with sharp stabbing pains in the hip joint and a sudden feeling of weakness

when you take a step. Alternatively, strained muscles or tendons produce aches in the hip during and after exercise. In all hip injuries, pain usually increases with movement, and the whole joint area is tender to touch.

Hip injuries tend to occur when lower limbs are placed under heavy stress. Running up hills and practicing sprint starts are the typical cause. To strengthen the hip, try the following exercise:

- Lie on your uninjured side, with your lower leg bent at a right angle for stability and the top leg straight.

- Slowly lift your top leg straight up to your side, until you can lift it no further. Hold it in the raised position for five seconds, then lower it slowly to the floor.

- Repeat fifteen times.

BACK INJURIES

Both jumping and throwing competitors are at risk for back injuries. The back undergoes extreme twisting forces during field events. Muscles are easily ruptured, and even the spine itself can be damaged. A doctor should always be seen for back injuries, because some can be very serious.

The most common injury is pulled back muscles. Its main symptom is severe pain in the lower back, made worse through movement or lifting. Treat initially with complete rest, lying down as much as possible on a firm supportive surface. Drawing your knees up with the feet flat on the surface will ease the pain by pushing the small of the back down onto the bed for support. As the pain diminishes, introduce light exercise to increase flexibility and strength.

5
Nutrition and Supplements

Understanding the Words

A **nutritionist** is an expert in nutrition; she can help you put together a healthy diet that is right for your body's needs.

If you do something in **moderation**, you don't do too much of it or too little; you keep to the middle.

Synthesis is the process of putting something together.

If something is **fortified** it has been made stronger (or more nutritious) than normal.

Although practice and training are an important part of being safe and successful in track-and-field, you also need to think about what you take into your body. Athletes must be careful to eat a proper blend of nutrients to make sure their bodies and minds perform as well as they possibly can. This doesn't just mean eating healthy foods but also choosing when to eat, how much to eat, and whether to take dietary supplements. Of course, when you choose a new diet or supplements, you should consult with a **nutritionist**, doctor, or some other expert. Don't make up your own nutrition program!

What to Eat

While a balanced diet is important for everyone, it is even more important for athletes. Typically an athlete has to eat considerably more than other people

Fruits and vegetables are important parts of a balanced diet.

CHOLESTEROL

A lot of bad things have been said about cholesterol—but most of this bad press is focused on LDLs, or low-density lipoproteins, which are a kind of cholesterol that can clog our blood vessels and make our hearts work harder. Our bodies make this cholesterol out of saturated fats, such as those found in animal fat from meats, butter, and whole milk. However, there is a kind of cholesterol known as HDLs, or high-density lipoproteins, which have a good effect on the body. Increasing your HDL levels can be as easy as exercising regularly.

do. The United States Food and Drug Administration (FDA) suggests that the average American should eat about 2,000 calories a day; for a male high school- or college-level athlete, a 3,000 to 4,000 calorie diet is more common. There are three main food groups to consider when choosing a diet: carbohydrates, protein, and fats.

CARBOHYDRATES

Carbohydrates are foods rich in a chemical called starch, which is what the body breaks down to get energy. Starchy foods include breads and grains; vegetables such as potatoes; cereal; pasta; and rice. Roughly half an athlete's calories should come from carbohydrates, but you should beware of heavily processed carbohydrates such as sugary foods and white bread made with bleached flour. These foods are quickly broken down into sugars, which the body processes into fats if it does not immediately burn them off. The best

TRACK & FIELD

carbohydrate choices for an athlete are pasta and whole-grain foods, as well as starchy vegetables, with vitamins as well as carbohydrates. A balanced diet avoids the "empty calories" supplied by white bread and sugars.

PROTEIN

Proteins are important chemicals found in all living things; these chemicals are used to perform specific functions inside our body cells. Each protein is a long, folded, chain-like molecule made up of "links" called amino acids. Our bodies can break down proteins that are found in foods into their base amino acids and use them to build new proteins that make up our muscles and bones. For this reason, during any exercise regimen, it is important to eat

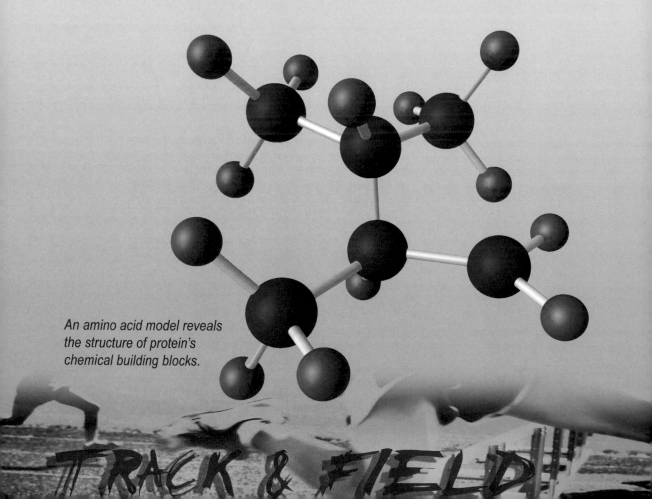

An amino acid model reveals the structure of protein's chemical building blocks.

enough protein to give the body the building blocks it needs to become stronger. The best sources of proteins are meats and dairy products (such as milk or cheese), as well as eggs and certain vegetables (such as soy, beans, and rice). A good rule of thumb for how much protein to eat is that the number of grams should be equal to about one-third of your body weight in pounds. For example, a 200-pound person should eat about 70 grams of protein every day, or a 120-pound person should have roughly 40 grams of protein.

FATS

Lots of times, we think of fats as bad for us, since eating too much of them is unhealthy. However, fat is an important ingredient needed to make our bodies work correctly. Without fats, our bodies cannot absorb certain vitamins as well as they should. Also, our skin and hair need some amount of fat to grow correctly. However, fats should still be eaten in **moderation**—no more than 70 grams a day. The best sources of fat are vegetable oils, olive oil, and nuts. Many foods contain saturated fats, which lead to the formation of cholesterol and force your heart to work harder.

Dietary Supplements

Many track-and-field athletes seek to improve their performance by taking dietary supplements, which are pills or drinks that contain nutrients or chemicals to improve their physical health or performance in the game. Dietary supplements do not include illegal performance-enhancing drugs. Instead, they contain vitamins and minerals, or chemicals that help the body use vitamins more efficiently. Although when properly used supplements can improve overall health and performance, you should always consult a doctor or other expert before taking them. Some examples of common supplements include vitamin tablets, creatine, and protein shakes or powder.

STAYING HYDRATED

The best diet in the world is no good if you become dehydrated. Dehydration occurs when your body doesn't have enough water, leading to fatigue, dizziness, and headaches, all of which can hurt your performance when playing. It's best to carry a bottle of water with you for the whole day before a practice or event to make sure that you are fully hydrated. In addition, you should be drinking water throughout the event to avoid becoming dehydrated as you sweat. Staying fully hydrated has many benefits besides helping your performance in the game—it can help concentration, improve digestive health, and reduce the risk of kidney stones.

VITAMIN TABLETS

For many reasons, we do not always get the vitamins and nutrients we need. Often, this is because our diets are not as balanced as they should be. Sometimes, it is because the foods that are available to us have been processed in such a way that they lose nutrients. Also, exhausted soil all over the country means that fruits and vegetables are sometimes not as nutrient-rich as they should be. In many cases, we can get the vitamins we need from vitamin supplements. These supplements, which are usually taken as a pill, sometimes contain a balanced mixture of vitamins and nutrients (known as multivitamins), and sometimes they contain a single vitamin or mineral that our diet is lacking. It is possible to overdose on certain vitamins, however, so be careful when taking supplements. Don't assume that because a little of

something is good for you that a lot of it will be better! Vitamins and minerals don't work that way. And always talk to your doctor before beginning to take supplements of any kind.

CREATINE

Creatine is a specific protein that is naturally found in your body's muscle cells. When taken in larger doses than is found in the body, creatine has the effect of increasing the rate of protein **synthesis** within your body cells. What this means is that you will have more energy to exercise, and you will see a greater improvement in strength and speed when you do exercise. However, pulling any chemical into your body can have negative effects as well, and you should talk to a doctor before beginning to take creatine. What's more, creatine is only suited for adult athletes, so young people (those under the age of 17) should not take it.

ATHLETICS AND ALCOHOL

After a big victory, teammates may be tempted to celebrate with alcohol. They may also be tempted to use alcohol to ease the pain of defeat. But alcohol intake can interfere with the body's recovery process, and this may interfere with your next performance.

It's especially important to avoid any alcohol 24 hours after exercise if you have any soft tissue injuries or bruises. Alcohol and injuries are a bad combination—it may actually increase swelling and bleeding, delaying the healing process.

AMY YODER BEGLEY

Since beginning her college career over a decade ago, Amy Yoder Begley continues to shine through her performance on the track. In 2000, she was the NCAA Indoor track champion in the 5000m race, and just a year later, she grabbed the same title for the Outdoor championships. Amy now competes for Team USA, and her professional career highlights include 2009 USA Outdoor 10,000m champion, and Indoor 3,000m champion in the same year. In 2008, she placed third at the Olympic Trials, and performed in Beijing, placing twenty-sixth overall. Begley is currently ranked sixth in the world—number one in the U.S. in the 10,000m race. Amy has accomplished all this while living with Celiac disease, which prevents her from consuming the protein gluten, found in bread, pasta, and many other foods containing wheat, barley, or rye.

PROTEIN SUPPLEMENTS

Getting enough protein from the food you eat can be difficult. Eating protein immediately after a workout is recommended (in order to refuel your body), but most people don't feel up to cooking or preparing themselves a meal immediately after a workout. That's why protein shakes are often a convenient choice. Many shakes contain blends of protein, carbohydrates, and fats, and some include vitamins, to help balance an athlete's diet. Furthermore, having protein immediately after a workout can help repair the damage sustained by

your muscles during the workout. However, you should remember that while protein shakes are useful for supplementing your diet, they should not be used to replace a normal food in any significant quantities. You can get plenty of nutrients from a balanced diet that cannot be replaced by artificial protein shakes, regardless of how **fortified** they may be. A nutritionist can tell you how to fit protein or supplement shakes into your diet safely and effectively.

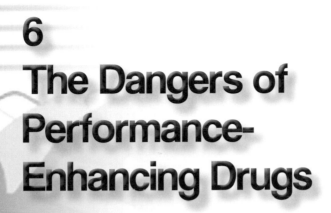

6

The Dangers of Performance-Enhancing Drugs

Understanding the Words

Infertility *means the inability to produce sperm or eggs; someone who is infertile cannot have biological children.*

An **electrolyte** *is a salt or mineral that conducts electrical impulses in the body, which is necessary for good health.*

If you have a **potassium deficiency**, *you lack enough potassium—one of the body's necessary electrolytes—to be healthy.*

Hormones *are the chemicals in your body that control and regulate the activity of many body systems.*

Insomnia *is a condition that makes it difficult to fall asleep or stay asleep.*

Hypertension *is the medical term for high blood pressure.*

Hallucinations *are when a person sees something that is not really there.*

Sadly, not all aspects of track-and-field are always positive or glamorous—even if you are a professional athlete. If you follow sports, you have most likely heard of athletes who use steroids and the controversy that surrounds them. By definition, performance-enhancing drugs are any form of chemicals that are taken in order to improve physical strength. While this may seem like a foolproof way to succeed in track-and-field, it is actually much more complicated than that. Not only are there legal consequences, there are also serious health issues that can result from steroid use.

Marion Jones is without a doubt one of the most well-known female track-and-field athletes of all time. She was suspected for many years of steroid use, but Jones repeatedly denied any involvement with illegal drug use. When Marion competed in Sydney, Australia, in 2000, at her first Olympic Games, she blew the competition away, returning home with three gold medals and two bronze—a first for female athletes. Steroid rumors continued to follow her, however, and she finally tested positive for performance-enhancing drug use and admitted lying to federal prosecutors about her situation. In the end, in 2007, Jones was stripped of all five of her Olympic medals and sentenced to six months in prison. Her story proves that performance-enhancing drugs simply aren't worth it!

Anabolic-Androgenic Steroids

Anabolic-androgenic steroids are usually taken to increase muscle mass. The main natural steroid produced by the body is testosterone, which causes muscle mass and male secondary characteristics, such as facial hair. Athletes take steroids such as methyl testosterone and oxymetholone in order to build muscle and recover from workouts. Since these drugs are illegal for athletes to use, beginning in 2002, "designer" drugs such as tetrahydrogestrinone (THG) have been created that allow athletes to be tested for steroid use without registering positive.

Marion Jones suffered personal and professional consequences as a result of her steroid use.

TRACK & FIELD

Many of these drugs are so new that they have not been tested thoroughly. Early indications are that these steroids may have serious side effects in men that range from baldness to growth of breasts, shrunken testicles, and **infertility**. Women tend to develop increased body hair, a deeper voice, and baldness. Both men and women may develop severe acne, liver abnormalities and tumors, cholesterol abnormalities, aggressive behavior, drug dependence, and future health risks. As of today, taking anabolic-androgenic steroids is illegal for enhancing sports performance, and they are outlawed in competition.

Diuretics

Diuretics are a class of drugs that increases urine production. Some athletes also believe that diuretics help them pass drug testing, since they dilute the urine. However, taking diuretics can upset the body's **electrolyte** balance and lead to dehydration. Taking diuretics such as Acetazolamide (Diamox) can lead to muscle cramps, exhaustion, dizziness, **potassium deficiency**, a drop in blood pressure, and even death.

Androstenedione

Androstenedione is a hormone produced naturally by the adrenal glands, ovaries, and testes, which is then converted to testosterone and estradiol, the human sex **hormone**. Artificially produced androstenedione is a controlled substance that is illegal in competition in the United States, though it is still being sold.

Scientific evidence suggests that androstenodione doesn't actually promote muscle growth, and it has several risks. In men, side effects include acne, diminished sperm production, shrunken testicles, and enlargement of breasts. In women, the drug causes acne and masculinization, such as growth

of facial hair. Androstenedione has also been shown to increase the chances of heart attack and stroke because it causes buildup of bad cholesterol.

Stimulants

Stimulants are a class of drugs that increase breathing rate, heart rate, and blood circulation. Athletes believe that these drugs stimulate their central nervous system, allowing them to perform better. Stimulants such as caffeine, cold remedies, and street drugs (cocaine and methamphetamine) can promote alertness, suppress appetite, and increase aggressiveness. However, these drugs can also make an athlete have difficulty concentrating, as well as produce insomnia, nervousness, and irritability. Athletes can even become psychologically and physically addicted. Other side effects include weight loss, tremors, heart rate abnormalities, hypertension, hallucinations, and heart attacks.

Over-the-Counter Drugs

Besides these dangerous and often illegal drugs, athletes also use painkillers and sedatives to enhance their performance. Painkillers allow athletes to operate with a higher level of pain tolerance, while sedatives can allow athletes to concentrate under stressful situations. However, both these drugs can also decrease performance—and they can disqualify an athlete from competing if they're detected in her bloodstream.

The Consequences of Performance-Enhancing Drug Use

Track-and-field athletes, like all other athletes, are often looking for a greater competitive edge to gain fame, acclaim, or an award or prize. However, there

is no magical concoction that will automatically bring these rewards. Instead, these performance-enhancing drugs tend to have many adverse side effects that could harm the body and its performance more than they can help.

The United States Anti-Doping Agency, or USADA monitors and oversees all illegal-substance use in track-and-field. Consequences for a positive test can vary from athlete to athlete, depending on the situation, but in general, here are the following penalties for an athlete who has committed a doping violation:

1. A first offense using a stimulant is a public warning, a disqualification from the event in which the sample was taken, and a loss of any award or prize money received.
2. A second offense for stimulant use is a 2-year period of ineligibility.
3. A third offense is a lifetime ban.

For the use of anabolic steroids, certain amphetamines or prohibited techniques, the consequences are as follows:

1. A first offense is a 2-year period of ineligibility.
2. A second offense is a lifetime ban.

The National Collegiate Athletic Association, or NCAA, also has very strict consequences for drug use. It sponsors two drug-testing programs, and both are required for every institution that is part of the association. Athletes are tested during NCAA Championships as well as randomly throughout the year. Not only are college athletes forbidden from taking steroids, but they are not allowed to take a variety of other drugs: anti-estrogens, diuretics, stimulants, peptide hormones, analogues, as well as any and all street drugs. In fact, the

NCAA's list of banned drugs includes more substances than those that are illegal according to federal law. If a NCAA athlete tests positive on a drug test, the student is banned from competing in any intercollegiate sport for an entire academic year, and loses one of his four years of eligibility. On the second offense, however, the athlete is banned indefinitely from all NCAA sports with no exceptions.

So the message here is clear: if you want to be an athlete, stay away from drugs! You will never get the same satisfaction out of a race in which you cheated to win, as you would from a win where you worked hard, pushed yourself mentally and physically, and gave it your all. As world-famous runner Steve Prefontaine once said, "to give anything less than your best is to sacrifice the gift."

Further Reading

ASEP. *Coaching Youth Track & Field*. Champaign, Ill.: Human Kinetics, 2008.

Bowerman, Bill and Bill Freeman. *Bill Bowerman's High-Performance Training for Track & Field*. Monterey, Calif.: Coaches Choice, 2008.

Cissik, John M. *Strength Training for Track-and-field*. Los Altos, Calif.: Tafnews Press, 2003.

Dunn, George D. *The Throws Manual*. Los Altos, Calif.: Tafnews Press, 2003.

Fishpool, Sean. *Beginner's Guide to Long Distance Running*. Hauppauge, N.Y.: Barron's Educational Series, 2005.

Jacoby, Ed. *Winning Jumps and Pole Vault*. Champaign, Ill.: Human Kinetics, 2009.

Lasorsa, Rob and James Peterson. *101 Shot Put Drills*. Monterey, Calif.: Coaches Choice, 2008.

Price, Robert. *Ultimate Guide to Weight Training for Track & Field*. Sportsworkout.com, 2007.

USA Track & Field. *USA Track & Field Coaching Manual*. Champaign, Ill.: Human Kinetics, 2000.

Find Out More on the Internet

Complete Track & Field
www.completetrackandfield.com

ESPN
espn.go.com/espn/wire?sportId=1700

Everything Track & Field
www.everythingtrackandfield.com

International Association of Athletics Federations
www.iaaf.org

Runner's World
www.runnersworld.com

The School Athletics Center—Track & Field
www.edgate.com/school_athletics/student/track_&_field

Track & Field News
www.trackandfieldnews.com

USA Track & Field
www.usatf.org

Disclaimer

The websites listed on this page were active at the time of publication. The publisher is not responsible for websites that have changed their address or discontinued operation since the date of publication. The publisher will review and update the websites upon each reprint.

Bibliography

About.com. "Fast and Slow Twitch Muscle Fibers," sportsmedicine.about. com/od/anatomyandphysiology/a/MuscleFiberType.htm, (24 March 2010).

About.com. "Muscle Fiber," backandneck.about.com/od/m/g/musclefiber. htm, (5 April 2010).

Bleacher Report. "The 10 Most Notorious Steroid Users in Sports History," bleacherreport.com/articles/155381-top-ten-notorious-steroid-users#page/8, (7 April 2010).

Body Building.com. "Track & Field Warmup Tips & Drills," www.bodybuild-ing.com/fun/eteam19.htm, (24 March 2010).

IAAF. "Bolt again! 9.58 World record in Berlin!" berlin.iaaf.org/news/kind=100/newsid=53047.html, (24 March 2010).

ibiblio. "Who Were the Celts?" www.ibiblio.org/gaelic/celts.html, (24 March 2010).

Intelius. "Tatyana Lysenko," search.intelius.com/Tatyana-Lysenko, (22 March 2010).

Maps of World. "Hammer Throw for Men at Olympics," www.mapsofworld. com/olympics/athletic-events/hammer-throw-for-men.html, (22 March 2010).

MedicineNet.com. "Definition of Gluteus maximus," www.medterms.com/script/main/art.asp?articlekey=25482, (5 April 2010).

TRACK & FIELD

NCAA. "NCAA Drug Testing," www.ncaa.org/wps/portal/ncaahome?WCM_GLOBAL_CONTEXT=/ncaa/ncaa/media+and+events/press+room/current+issues/drug+testing, (7 April 2010).

newFitness.com. "Forms of Aerobic Exercises," www.new-fitness.com/Aerobics/types.html, (24 March 2010).

SpeedEndurance.com. "Pole Vault World Records should be Modified," speedendurance.com/2009/08/21/pole-vault-world-records-should-be-modified, (24 March 2010).

Sports Definitions.com. "Athletics," www.sportsdefinitions.com/terms-by-sport.php (24 March 2010).

USATF. "Amy Yoder Begley," www.usatf.org/athletes/bios/BegleyAmy.asp (5 April 2010).

USATF. "Antidoping, Frequently Asked Questions," www.usatf.org/about/legal/antidoping/FAQ.asp#Q3, (7 April 2010).

TRACK & FIELD

Index

Picture Credits

Able, Glen: p. 50
Bran, Creative Commons: p. 19
Cienpies Design & Communication, Dreamstime: p. 74
Creative Commons: pp. 11, 12, 15, 21, 61
Deal, Bobby; Dreamstime: p. 49
Faivre-Duboz, Thomas; Creative Commons: p. 85
Kleszczu, Creative Commons: p. 14
Laczay, Bjorn; Creative Commons: p. 24
Martin, T.D.; Dreamstime: p. 52
Mtsiri, Dreamstime: p. 60
Prole, Ivan: p. 34
Proskuryakov, Ivan; Dreamstime: p. 76
Scroch, Creative Commons: p. 32
Thompson, Christy; Dreamstime: p. 46
Tivedshambo, Creative Commons: p. 22
U.S. Airforce: p. 42
U.S. Navy: pp. 17, 29, 45, 58

To the best knowledge of the publisher, all images not specifically credited are in the public domain. If any image has been inadvertently uncredited, please notify Harding House Publishing Service, 220 Front Street, Vestal, New York 13850, so that credit can be given in future printings.

About the Author and the Consultants

Gabrielle Vanderhoof attends Binghamton University in upstate New York. She is a former competitive figure skater who hopes to have a career in publishing public relations. This is her first time writing for Mason Crest.

Susan Saliba, Ph.D., is a senior associate athletic trainer and a clinical instructor at the University of Virginia in Charlottesville, Virginia. A certified athletic trainer and licensed physical therapist, Dr. Saliba provides sports medicine care, including prevention, treatment, and rehabilitation for the varsity athletes at the university. Dr. Saliba is a member of the national Athletic Trainers' Association Educational Executive Committee and its Clinical Education Committee.

Eric Small, M.D., a Harvard-trained sports medicine physician, is a nationally recognized expert in the field of sports injuries, nutritional supplements, and weight management programs. He is author of *Kids & Sports* (2002) and is Assistant Clinical professor of pediatrics, Orthopedics, and Rehabilitation Medicine at Mount Sinai School of Medicine in New York. He is also Director of the Sports Medicine Center for Young Athletes at Blythedale Children's Hospital in Valhalla, New York. Dr. Small has served on the American Academy of Pediatrics Committee on Sports Medicine, where he develops national policy regarding children's medical issues and sports.